Birth Out

The Journey of Discovering Your
God-Given Purpose

by

LaTonya Parsons

Copyright © 2024 – Birth Out: The Journey of Discovering Your God-Given Purpose by LaTonya Parsons

All rights reserved. No part of this book may be reproduced or transmitted in any form, or by any electronic or mechanical means, without prior written consent of the publisher, the author, or an editor.

Book Cover Design: Rose Miller

Editor – Coach Jacqueline of Penned Just Write LLC

Publishing Company: Tall Paul Publications

Paperback ISBN: 978-0-9835794-9-6

Acknowledgements

In the culmination of this literary journey, I am humbled to extend my deepest gratitude to those who have been instrumental in bringing "Birth Out: The Journey of Discovering Your God-Given Purpose" to fruition.

To My Beloved Husband: My heartfelt appreciation goes to my wonderful husband, whose unwavering support has been the bedrock of my endeavors. Your encouragement and belief in me have fueled my passion, and for that, I am profoundly grateful.

To My Precious Children, Faith, and Josiah: Your presence in my life is a continuous wellspring of inspiration. You both are a constant reminder of the importance of the journey we are all on. You both unknowingly propel me to strive for excellence, and I am blessed to be your parent.

To My Amazing Family: A sincere thank you to my extended family for being a constant source of strength and encouragement. Your presence in life's highs and lows has made this endeavor more meaningful. Your unwavering support has been a guiding light.

To My Sister, Vicky: A special acknowledgment is reserved for my sister. Your persistent encouragement and belief in my writing abilities has echoed in my ears for years. This book stands as a testament to your nudges and reminders. Sis, it is finally here, and I am immensely grateful for your influence.

To the Almighty: Above all, I extend my deepest gratitude to the Lord, the giver of all gifts. Thank you for entrusting me with the beautiful and profound gift of "Birth Out." Your guidance, inspiration, and divine hand have shaped every word on these pages. I am honored to share this work with the world as a testament to Your grace and purpose as I reflect on the support, encouragement, and inspiration received.

Table of Contents

Acknowledgements iii
Introduction vii

Chapter 1
Pregnant with Purpose 11

Chapter 2
When the Journey does not Make Sense 17

Chapter 3
The Confirmation 23

Chapter 4
Pain is Part of the Process 27

Chapter 5
What does it Mean to be Birthed Out? 31

Chapter 6
Is This Part of the Pain? 35

Chapter 7
The Promise in the Midst of Chaos 41

Chapter 8
Reunited and it is ALL Good – When your Yes meets His Will 45

Chapter 9
Repositioning 49

Chapter 10
It's All Worth It 55

Chapter 11
   Uniquely You 59

Chapter 12
   The Journey Continues 61

Bonus #1
   The Delivery Room 63

Bonus #2
   Walking in It 65

About the Author 67

Introduction

Thank you so much for being here. Honestly, this marks my third attempt at writing this book and I'm determined to make it the first of many best sellers. It's probably unnecessary for me to mention this, but I believe it's important for the sake of our collective journey. Some of you reading may have pursued different paths in the past—going back to school, earning a degree, starting a business, or entering the world of ministry. When pursuing a path, one often encounters life's challenges, which can make progress feel like an uphill battle. However, I declare over your life that this time will not be like the last. This time, you will finish. So, here we are, finishing together. Thank God for His grace. I'm thrilled that you've joined me. My prayer is that as you delve into my life experiences, you'll discern God in yours. Timing is crucial, but God's timing is perfect. I pray that as you read, you give birth. Give birth to what? Purpose. I pray that as you read, the words on the page come alive and transport you to another world. My prayer is that as you read, you find comfort and strength in the words. Thus, I know that this is not just a book; it is a Kingdom experience. I am so excited about what God is doing in and through you.

Now, let's explore how this book operates. It's not about how you read it, but more so about your active engagement. Embedded in each chapter is a Birth Out Activation Section that will revisit some of your life experiences. Through my story, I pray you can now see God's hand at work in your story. Pace yourself and allow the Holy Spirit to minister to you. Remember, you are not in this alone. As we travel this journey together, know that I am here with you, cheering you on and celebrating the amazing ways in which God will work in your life. To be clear, this is not just a narrative of actions but an exercise in fully embracing who God has called you to be. I will be your guide, so here we grow.

What is Birth Out?

What's within me? Why was I born? What is my purpose? Why am I different? What is the reason for all the things I have been through? These are just a few of the questions we ask ourselves. The answer is simple: God has impregnated you with a holy seed.

However, there is a lot of preparation that needs to be done prior to the delivery. According to *Luke 1:31-35*, an Angel informed Mary she was carrying the Messiah, the Savior of the world. But, how could this be, considering she had never been intimate with a man? The Holy Ghost was to impart and deposit the Holy Seed. She didn't have to name Him; it was predetermined that He would be called Jesus. All Mary had to do was carry Him. And you, like Mary, have been impregnated with a holy seed, and you have been carrying it your whole life. Yes, you were born because of it. God did not decide on your purpose once you came into the earth. You were born on purpose, and pregnant with purpose. Our God is intentional. So, this holy seed has been in you the whole time. All the experiences you have gone through have been to prepare for its arrival. Therefore, we find ourselves in the present moment. What actions will you take in light of this newfound information? This is why you are reading this book. Let's go on this journey of being BIRTHED OUT together.

Being "Birthed Out" is not a one-time action. It is a lifestyle that every believer is called to achieve. The process in Chapter 5 allows God to accomplish His divine purpose in you. This process is as unique to each individual as our DNA is. It is specific to you and the holy investment; your God-given purpose that God has deposited in you. It's surprising how many people live without allowing the Holy Spirit to fully work in their lives and, therefore, cannot fully manifest the purpose that God had for them. I am confident that this is not the case for you. That is why you were led to read this book. God has begun a good work in you, and He desires to complete it. After reading this book, many of you will never be the same. Things will shift. The Master has summoned you to take part in the Birth Out process and I pray that you may truly feel the presence of God in your life like never before. God has been present throughout the entire journey. We often overlook the power of His hand in our lives until we find ourselves in need of His help. Truth is, God has been getting you ready for your purpose throughout your entire life. Every experience you have had in your life can and will bring Him glory. Yes, the good, the bad, and the ugly. It will all work out for the good.

> *[31] And, behold, thou shalt conceive in thy womb, and bring forth a son, and shalt call his name Jesus. 32 He shall be great, and shall be called the Son of the Highest: and the Lord God shall give unto him the throne of his father David: 33 And he shall reign over the house of Jacob forever; and of his kingdom there shall be no end. 34 Then said Mary unto the angel, How shall this be, seeing I know not a man? 35 And the angel answered and said unto her, The Holy Ghost shall come upon thee, and the power of the Highest shall overshadow thee: therefore also that holy thing which shall be born of thee shall be called the Son of God. Luke 1:31-35 (KJV)*

Chapter 1

Pregnant with Purpose

What does it mean to be pregnant with purpose? What is our purpose? Where does it come from? How do we manifest it? These profound questions find their resounding answers to God's predetermined plan for each one of us. *Jeremiah 1:5* boldly declares that even before Jeremiah's birth, God had called and ordained him. Remarkably, this divine calling extends to you. God has called, chosen, and equipped each of us for our purpose long before our earthly existence. Hence, we are here because of purpose — precisely, His purpose. As we entered this earthly realm, we were birthed with purpose, already intricately woven into the fabric of our being.

One of the adversary's most insidious tactics is to deceive us into believing we lack a divine purpose. He endeavors to persuade us that we are here by accident, and that God does not have the perfect plan for us. Contrary to this deception, *Jeremiah 29:11* reassures us that God's thoughts toward us are benevolent, promising us a future with an expected end. God harbors good thoughts for His children. Therefore, being pregnant with purpose is not a realization that begins only when we consciously acknowledge it. It is a reality that began before our awareness, even before our earthly existence. God had us on His mind, fashioning a divine purpose for our existence.

As I promised, this book will contain some insights into my personal journey. Together, we will explore several years of my life, and I pray that in doing so, you will be blessed and come to acknowledge the unwavering presence of God that has directed your path since the very beginning. While it may sound cliché, it holds truth. I have always had a sense of my uniqueness, knowing that I didn't quite fit in with any particular group. I had a noticeable presence from a very early age. However, I desperately wanted to just blend in. I quickly grasped the art of adaptation.

I want to go back to one of the earliest memories I have that will connect the idea of being pregnant with purpose. When I was about eight years old, a prophet (a person ordained by God to speak for him) came to our church to conduct a revival. I grew up attending a Pentecostal church. It was there that I received my foundation in holiness. My pastor, at the time, was such an amazing woman of God. When I was younger, I had many amazing men and women pour into my life, and it wasn't until later in adulthood that I truly understood the profound impact they had. Well, back to the story. I was unaware of the prophetic gift back then when the prophet called me up to the altar and prophesied over my life. This was the first time I ever remembered receiving words of prophecy. I can't even tell you if I knew what was going on, but I remember that day as if it was yesterday. "God has called you to be a blessing to women. He's put ministry inside of you", was his prophecy over me. He also prophesied how the presence of God within me would influence women's lives.

I didn't fully comprehend what that meant back then because the life experiences I was going through didn't align with the words being spoken over me. I experienced molestation by a family member at the age of eight, which caused me to develop an unhealthy connection with food. The Holy Spirit just recently made this connection known to me. He revealed to me that my initial relationship with food was not always unhealthy, but the molestation allowed for the development of distorted relationships.

Unbeknownst to me, God had planted a divine seed within me. My purpose. However, there was another seed, not of divine origin but from the enemy, that was also attempting to grow. It took many years to recognize, identify, and uproot that destructive seed. I want to highlight that while God fills us with a sense of purpose, the enemy also tries to sow seeds that undermine that purpose. He tries to assassinate the very seed God planted in us.

I hope that as we embark on this journey together, you will find meaning in your own life experiences. It's important to take breaks and contemplate your life. Yes, God has placed purpose within you, but what else has tried to take root? Is it a lack of confidence or self-doubt? What has tried to steal away your divine future? We will often take breaks to write and reflect on the insights inspired by the Holy Spirit.

We will dive deep into the various periods of your life. While it may be tough to go back to certain years, doing so is important for moving forward and finding healing. It's essential for the work to be completed within you so you can fulfill the full purpose of God. This is the path of self-discovery, where we acknowledge the abilities, talents, and higher purpose that reside within us. These are not only meant for us to see but also for the world to witness and find their way back to God.

Expect many pauses along the way and embrace them. Our purpose resides within us, occasionally nudging us to remind us of its presence. It shows up even when we feel we're in the wrong place or not in the best relationship with God. Respond to the internal nudges and discomfort that signal you're off track from your intended path. You are called to more. There is a divine assignment for you, given by God. It's time to answer the call of our purpose. So, ready or not, it's time to give birth.Top of Form

Birth Out Activation Section: The Purification Process

One common mistake people often make is avoiding the confrontation of unresolved issues. Regardless of being chosen and anointed, it is important to consider the challenges or issues that you may have been neglecting or, even better, not dealing with. What you carry within will eventually be delivered, encompassing both the positive and negative aspects. As carriers, the initial step is to recognize the inner workings within our spiritual womb. Failure to address these issues now may lead to repercussions later on. It's crucial to recognize that even in ministry, one can grapple with unresolved problems. Let's address these issues proactively. What have you been wrestling with? Identify your greatest struggles, and honestly list them here.

This is the moment to delve deep into your life, exploring your most significant obstacle. Resist the urge to linger in this place; instead, allow yourself to confront and uncover whatever has been a major hindrance. Invite the Holy Spirit to bring these issues to the surface, freeing you from the need to hide or conceal them any longer. Allow the Holy Spirit to guide you to the incidents or events when these seeds were planted. Addressing only the branches won't suffice; it's crucial to uproot and destroy the roots. The question is, are you willing to let Him do it? Remember, you've come too far to get stuck here. Whether it takes minutes, hours, days or longer, persist until the process is complete. God has profound plans for you, so trust in His transformative process — it will be worthwhile.

Prayer

Thank you for the holy deposit within me, Lord. Holy Spirit, assist me in this process. Reveal any blockages or unresolved issues that I may not have dealt with. I stand naked and exposed before you, desiring to be used by you. Lord, have your way in my life.

In Jesus' name, Amen.

Scripture Reading: Psalm 139

Chapter 2

When the Journey does not Make Sense

I've experienced the feeling of confusion, as it seemed like my life was heading in the opposite direction of the way I believed God wanted me to go. It's intriguing how, from our perspective, certain experiences seem miles away from our destined path. Our thoughts often diverge from God's, and there are moments when things don't make sense to us, but they make perfect sense to God.

In my early twenties, I was engaged to be married, firmly believing it was in line with God's will. However, later revelations proved otherwise. It's important to recognize that sometimes we don't know what God has for us. Sometimes we simply miss the mark. The challenge arises when we cling to what God hasn't approved, trying to hold on to it even after we know that it isn't part of His plan or only meant to be seasonal. The problem lies in not aligning ourselves with God's intended path for our lives, kicking against His will. He will always show us signs and give warnings when we veer off course. It is then up to us to heed these signs and warnings and take the necessary action.

I received many signs that the relationship I was in wasn't for me. I was called up front during a service and it was prophesied that I would be heartbroken. I remember the words, "I see you crying". I convinced myself that this wasn't a message from God and the prophet was off. I soon found out that it was a direct warning from our loving Father. I also had a dream about how the relationship would end. Sure, enough it ended as confirmed in the dream. Even then, I still tried to hold on. I was convinced God was making a mistake when it came to this relationship that I wanted so badly. However, it just wasn't His will for me. During that season in my life, nothing seemed to make sense anymore. I thought I had it all figured out, but God had other plans.

The beauty of things that make little sense to us is that they make complete sense to God. [1]Romans 8:28 is one of my favorite Bible verses, reminding us that all things work together for good for those who love the Lord and are called according to His purpose. Even when life seems out of alignment, God is in control, orchestrating everything for our good.

During that relationship, where I struggled to let go, God turned the situation around. Despite the initial devastation of the breakup, that season became one of the best experiences of my life because it drew me closer to God. In those dark times, I felt God's presence in a profound way and discovered that He is near to the brokenhearted.

So, if you're facing something that doesn't make sense right now, understand that your steps are ordered by God. Your seemingly confusing path will work out to be the very one that leads to your divine destiny. God has ordained this way

---

1. Romans 8:28 And we know that all things work together for good to them that love God, to them who are the called according to his purpose.

for you. Trust in Him, fully and completely, for He knows the way you take *Job 23:10.*

Praising God even when things don't make sense is a profound expression of trust in God. Learning how to give thanks in everything aligns with the will of God in Christ Jesus concerning us. Your experiences, like the difficult period I experienced, reflect the paradox of God's ways, often defying our human logic.

My family moved to a new state a few years ago, yet another example of a time where things did not make sense to me. Everything at the time seemed to point towards staying put – with my kids in high school and my dream job secured – God's plan beckoned us to go. This decision was tough, to say the least. It required a profound trust in God, leading to a heightened dependence on Him for everything. I thought I had faith, but during this process, I learned that my faith wasn't where I thought it was. I learned He is my source and my family's source. Yes, it was challenging at times, but God always showed Himself to be faithful. This move, though initially daunting, revealed the depth of my reliance on God and His unwavering provision. He never let me down.

Even when things don't seem to make sense, we can find assurance in the fact that God has our back. His plan, even if initially incomprehensible, eventually unfolds beautifully in His perfect timing. This serves as a reminder to stay firmly in the hands of the One who orchestrates all things for our good.

ಶುಭ ಶುಭ

Birth Out Activation Section: Purification Continues

I know things have come up since you started this journey that you thought you had dealt with. Dealing with issues and burying them are two very different things. Out of sight, out of mind, does not mean that it is gone. It means you choose not to deal with it. Today, I challenge you to pick up the spiritual mirror and take a good look at yourself. No, do not turn away so quickly. Take the time to take a good look. Yes, that is really you. Do you like what you see? Does your reflection look like Christ? If not, what must change? The Spirit is here to help you.

Many make it to this point and stop because it may be too painful or difficult to face. You have been led to this place for a reason. Now is the time to deal with the unresolved issues you continue to deal with. You may have to ask your parents what was going on around the time you were born. You may have to have a tough conversation with your mother about her pregnancy. If your parents are no longer here, just know God is. The Spirit can reveal ALL things. This is a tough journey, but well worth it. This may be the time where you need to seek professional help with some things that are coming up. Do not be ashamed to seek help and follow God's lead. He will never steer you wrong. There is greatness coming out of this, but you cannot skip steps. Every stage is essential.

What things are coming up that you need to address at this point?

When the Journey does not Make Sense ✠ 21

Prayer

Father God, Thank You for the opportunity to get things in my life right with you. Please help me deal with issues and emotions that I have hidden and buried. I admit, some things are too much for me to handle, so I'm asking for your help with these things. Please take me through this entire process. Thank you for your promise that you are always with me. I want my life to bring You Glory.

In Jesus' Name, Amen

Scripture Reading: Psalm 51

Chapter 3
The Confirmation

I Remember going through a season where I was earnestly seeking to know God's purpose for my life and what He had called me to be. During this intense period of searching, I devoted time to studying the Scriptures, praying, and fasting. I longed to uncover the purpose of my existence and the divine plan for my life. It was in this season that I gained clarity on God's plan for my life and discovered an intriguing connection to my past.

Having grown up attending church, I went to Sunday School, Bible Studies, and sang in the choir. During my later teenage years, I felt a hunger for a deeper understanding of God and His Word. As I delved into scripture, I encountered stories like Balaam and the talking donkey, Jephthah and his vow, and many others that fascinated me. While studying, I naturally began taking notes, not understanding their importance at that moment. It was a routine part of my study process, and I accumulated these notes in a binder over the years.

Fast forward to the season of seeking God's purpose. I remember praying one night in my bedroom. In a moment of divine revelation, I heard the Holy Spirit ask, "What hides beneath your bed?" Although I considered myself tidy, there was one thing beneath my bed — the binder of notes. As I picked it up, the Holy Spirit clearly conveyed, "Feed my sheep."

Now, I understand the speeches that I had to make, the mini messages that I delivered, and the church plays that I participated in. I was always called to be up front, even though that was not the place I desired to be. I preferred to be behind the scenes in the background. However, during my childhood, it was common for children to follow instructions obediently without questioning them. Little did I know these things were preparing me for the call.

This revelation confirmed God's call for me to preach the gospel. While I had a brief preview of the call, the full revelation was still waiting to be unveiled. As I reflect on this experience, it becomes clear to me that God's purpose for us is intricately intertwined with our lives, sometimes without our knowledge. Our passion and purpose are deeply connected, and God has a way of orchestrating every aspect of our life to fit perfectly into His divine plan. To those in search of confirmation regarding their purpose, I encourage you to reconsider and observe what you have been engaged in or feel strongly about. It is God who knows how to connect the dots and confirm your calling, making clear the purpose He has for you. I've learned that confirmation involves more than just the call. It's about understanding who we are. Embrace the certainty that God knows and will make clear exactly who He has called you to be.

Birth Out Activation Section:
Top of FormPurification – The Search

We have reached a juncture where our efforts are exhausted, and it is time to invite God to search our hearts. This phase might feel uneasy, as we are uncertain about what the Holy Spirit will unveil. Surrendering to the guidance of the Holy Spirit is necessary to explore hidden areas. Grant Him access to every room in your life, including the secret and deeply buried places. In this phase, the uncovering of generational curses and cycles may occur. It's important to recognize that the duration of this phase can differ for each person – some may experience it for days, weeks, or even months. Patience is key. Rushing the process may hinder the detailed work of the Holy Spirit.

Consider starting a journal to document your experiences, thoughts, and prayers as you go through this transformative process. Make sure your journal is easily accessible, as unexpected revelations may come up. As you engage in this introspective process, consider delving into *Psalm 139* for inspiration and guidance.

Reflect on the following questions: What revelations have emerged during this phase? Have you been able to identify life cycles or generational patterns? Share your thoughts here:

Prayer
Holy Spirit, I give you full access to my life. I have done all I can do and now I desperately need Your help. Here I am, naked and exposed. Do what only you can do, I give you permission. My desire is to reflect Christ.
In Jesus' Name, Amen
Scripture Reading: Psalm 139

Chapter 4
Pain is Part of the Process

Pain is an aspect of life that many people instinctively try to avoid. It is often unwelcome and viewed negatively. The inclination is to steer clear of it. However, understanding that pain is an integral part of the spiritual development process is crucial. Through pain, we gain a different perspective of God, and we learn to call upon Him as the ultimate solution. Though painful experiences are not something we desire, they are, in a sense, necessary. Pain pushes us to see God in ways that might otherwise be overlooked.

Consider the analogy of childbirth, where pain is an inherent part of the process. The discomfort is not easily avoidable but is crucial for the birth of a child. The advice given during childbirth: "When you feel the contractions, push," underscores the notion that painful as it may be, contractions serve a purpose – they contribute to the birthing process.

The same is true in our spiritual process. It is crucial to keep moving forward when we encounter difficulties, trials, and challenges. The challenge might lie in our consistent inability to comprehend the purpose behind our pain. When faced with pain during this journey, our instinctive reaction may be to withdraw, find shelter, or attempt to ease it. Drawing a parallel to childbirth, just as contractions signify impending birth, the pain we encounter holds the promise of new life.

Consider reflecting on the pain you've experienced during your life journey so far. Many of you have navigated through diverse and challenging situations, and each person's journey is unique. It's essential to acknowledge that, through it all, God is intimately present. He is Emmanuel *(God with us)*, and His promises assure us He will never leave or forsake us *(Deuteronomy 31:6)*. He is a present help in times of trouble *(Psalm 46:1)*, and He is with us always, even to the end of the world *(Matthew 28:20)*. By placing our trust in Him and understanding that pain is a natural part of the journey, we can confidently navigate through challenges with hope and faith. Recognize that pain is a producer. It serves the purpose of generating purpose.

Birth Out Activation Section: Give it to the Lord

Now is the perfect time to surrender all the things you have uncovered and addressed to God. Give them over to Him completely, putting an end to this chapter once and for all. These things will never haunt or torment you again. They were once a part of your past but are not welcome in your future. Imagine, if these issues weren't resolved now, they would have come up again in your ministry down the line. My prayer is that this is the last time you see these enemies attack your soul. Below, enumerate the things from which you have been liberated (e.g., low self-esteem, jealousy, selfishness, envy, pride).

This is your NEVER again list.

_____

_____

_____

_____

_____

_____

_____

_____

_____

Prayer

Dear Heavenly Father, here are things I have dealt with, but now I give them totally and completely to You, Lord. Cleanse me from the inside out. I am now ready to go through the Birth Out process unhindered and delivered from my past. Thank you for cleansing me, Father.

In Jesus' Name, Amen

Scripture Reading: Psalms 51

Chapter 5

What does it mean to be Birthed Out?

The concept of being "birthed out" originated over fifteen years ago when my then, pastor, asked me to lead a ministry at the church. He gave me the name "Birth Out" with no explanation. This was the usual behavior for my pastor. We would say that he trained using the Mr. Miyagi, from the Karate Kid Movie, method. At first, it didn't seem connected to anything, but later you would have a revelation. He did everything by faith and as we followed him, we learned what faith was all about. At first, this request puzzled me, but then I realized it was connected to my previous life experiences.

Months prior to this request, while preparing to minister at a church in Schenectady, NY, the Holy Spirit led me to examine *Luke 1:36-40*. Instead of viewing it as a Christmas story, I saw Mary as a prototype for the Church. Mary's journey became an analogy to the spiritual process of giving birth. This passage revealed that, like Mary, believers are pregnant with God's purpose, going through a personal, spiritual journey. I was in awe because I had never seen this passage like this before.

A few years earlier, during another ministry opportunity in Syracuse, NY, ironically, I was pregnant and received a clear, audible message from the Holy Spirit calling me a "spiritual midwife." This was right is the middle of my preaching. I wasn't sure what to do with this message, but I held it close to my heart. Although unfamiliar with the term "spiritual midwife", I understood it had to be part of my divine calling. Still, I could not make the connection.

Returning back to the Sunday when my pastor asked me to lead the ministry "Birth Out," I suddenly understood that every experience in my life had been leading up to this very moment. My pastor's request was the birthing of my ministry "Birth Out". Everything now made sense, like the prophecy at eight years old, the troubled relationship, the revelation of what was under my bed, the revelation in *Luke 1:35-39*, the Holy Spirit calling me a Spiritual Midwife, and many other experiences. It was all for the birthing of my purpose. I don't know if my pastor knew what he was asking me to do, but God used him to allow me to see WHO he had called me to be. Birth Out is a transformative journey of uncovering one's divine purpose and understanding God's plan for one's life. The term includes the notion that, just like Mary, those who have faith undergo a personal and spiritual journey of giving life to the purpose that God has placed within them. This journey is as unique as we are. It can be difficult and easily overlooked, yet it holds a divine purpose for each of us. I often encounter people who feel frustrated because they don't know their purpose and that is what *Birth Out* is here for. To help you see God in your own life. He alone can and will reveal His Divine plan for your life.

Birth Out Activation Section: Don't Skip Steps

Acknowledging the need for healing and going through the purification process are crucial steps in our Birth Out journey. Make sure to finish each step before proceeding to the next one. The emphasis is not on the speed at which we travel during the journey. Our goal is to allow the Holy Spirit to complete the work needed. If you're ready, let's continue.

Now, let's explore the realm of spiritual intimacy and worship where you can renew and strengthen the connection between your essence and the Father.

Worship is the sacred space where you can stand before God, fully exposed and unashamed. There's no need to hide or cover anything up because God sees and knows every part of you, yet loves you with an everlasting love. This is a time to embrace that love and express your gratitude to the Father for His boundless love.

Intimacy and worship are not occasional practices, but integral parts of our daily lives. Consider the various ways you commit to worshiping God daily and list them below.

_____

_____

_____

_____

Prayer

Father God, I love You with all that I am. Please help me connect with You intimately in worship every day. I thank You for loving me. My desire is to express my love to you in worship.

In Jesus' Name, Amen

Scripture Reading: John 15:1-8

Chapter 6

Is This Part of the Plan?

There are aspects of the Birth Out process that can be perplexing, often surpassing our human comprehension. We frequently yearn to have our lives meticulously planned out, only to discover that in the Birth Out process, our plans seldom align with God's. Many times, we endure challenges and face circumstances that appear to divert us from our perceived path. These detours in life lead us through unpaved roads, forests, the wilderness, valleys, and deserts. We may question whether this is what God had planned for us.

It's crucial to recognize that in these moments, we are grappling with the unknown. When we lack a clear understanding of God's ordained plan for our lives, we may find it challenging to discern our position within that plan. Personally, I spent a significant amount of time questioning the plan. Whether reflecting on childhood, adolescence, or early adulthood, things often seemed to deviate from what I perceived as God's divine plan.

One vivid memory takes me back to my early years of marriage, with two young children and a commitment to full-time ministry. Despite my sincere desire to please the Lord, the challenges I faced during this season seemed incongruent with any divine plan. Many individuals from the ministry we were part of supported us with blessings, such as food and shelter. Starting a family and working in ministry with limited resources required a deep reliance on God and His people. I had to learn to trust and depend on God in ways I hadn't experienced before. I had grown accustomed to working and having financial independence. Things were truly uncomfortable for me.

During those years, there was a Mother's Day when I couldn't afford to buy a pair of stockings, costing no more than a dollar or two. I remember crying and questioning what I had done wrong. I share this to encourage you to reflect on times in your life that may not have felt like part of God's plan. It may have seemed like you were abandoned, forgotten, or forsaken, but I want to assure you that this is not the case.

What I've discovered is that when we feel lost in the detours of life, it is often a crucial part of God's intricate plan for our growth, development, and preparation for the purpose He has planted within us. Trusting God during these uncertain times becomes a profound journey of faith, resilience, and ultimately, a deepening connection with Him.

It Is common to believe that our lives are deviating from the divine plan when we feel off-course. However, what I understand is that in those exact moments, we often find ourselves perfectly aligned with God's plan. It is during these times that we can know God intimately. During what may seem like detours or off-course experiences, God is actively birthing character within us. One aspect that we often overlook when talking about anointings and ministries.

Character and integrity are vital aspects that accompany anointing and ministry, and these qualities are often developed during seasons that feel like deviations from the expected path. I encourage you to ask God, "What are you developing in me during this season?" It may not align with your expectations, and it may not feel the way you expected, but it is in these moments that God is shaping the very characteristics that will sustain us as we walk out His plan and will for our lives.

I often reflect on one of my favorite scriptures, *Job 23:10*, which states, "For he knows the way that I take; when he has tested me, I will come forth as pure gold." God is aware of the path we are on, and through the refining process, He is molding us into something precious and valuable. He knows what He's doing in us, where He wants to take us, and when we need to get there. It is all part of His meticulous plan. So, stay the course, don't veer off track, trust God, and rest assured that you are secure in the center of His Will and in the palm of His hand.

Birth Out Activation Section: Practice healthy habits. Pray, Study, and Meditate on the Word!

Naturally, discovering what you are carrying in the early stages of pregnancy can be challenging. The waiting period can be uncomfortable and even frustrating. However, I bring great news for those who may feel impatient, as I can be sometimes, recognizing that God is still working on me. Your purpose in ministry was predestined before you came into this world. So, it's not just about discovering your calling; it's about it being revealed to you through the Holy Spirit. We will delve into this revelation later.

For now, let's direct our attention to the changes that are occurring within you. Since embarking on this journey, what transformations are you noticing? This might include alterations in sleep patterns, shifts in appetite, changes in social circles, or an increased hunger for God's Word. Take a moment to record these changes here:

_____

_____

_____

_____

_____

_____

Is This Part of the Plan?

Prayer

Father God, thank you for choosing me out of all the people in the world. I am profoundly grateful that you saw fit to invest in me. My utmost desire is to make you proud. I wholeheartedly commit to this journey and process, no matter how uncomfortable it may get. I draw strength from you, and I am thankful for your unwavering support.

In Jesus' name, I pray. Amen.

Scripture Reading: Jeremiah 1:5

Chapter 7

The Promise in the Midst of Chaos

We often expect a path that is clear from any obstacles. With God, His promises often manifest themselves amidst chaos, when everything appears disorderly, out of control, and when nothing seems to function. If we draw parallels to childbirth, one of the most beautiful miracles arises from what can seem like chaotic scenes.

The pain, difficulties, and discomfort associated often with pregnancy and childbirth all seem to dissipate once the baby is born. It is as if it never happened. Or is it that the joy of giving birth overshadows it all? Making it seem minuscule in comparison to the arrival of the long-awaited promise. The delivery room can be a hectic place with the doctors, nurses, family, and support persons. There is often a feeling of being overwhelmed by everything that is happening. This is sometimes how our spiritual journeys can seem.

Today, I want to encourage you not to interpret the surrounding chaos as an indicator of what God is doing within you. Many times, what's happening around us doesn't align with what God has spoken to us. This is why the Bible instructs us to walk by faith and not by sight, emphasizing that the things we see are temporary, but the unseen things are eternal. Therefore, we must change our perspective and employ a Kingdom mindset and vision to truly discern what God is doing. A Kingdom mindset focuses on God's rule and reign. It sees everything through that lens, knowing that God is in full control because we have surrendered our lives to Him. He, in turn, promises to take care of us as His children.

Do not let the craziness associated with birth to deter or distract you from the miraculous process that is unfolding. Today, I declare God will fulfill His promises in your life. You will witness the goodness of the Lord in the land of the living. Hold on to the promise, remember what God has spoken, for this season will give birth to it.

Chaos often serves as an indicator that we shouldn't push, but I want to encourage you to push, even during chaos. When it seems like you have too much on your plate, too much responsibility, and it feels overwhelming, that is the perfect sign that it's time for you to push. Even when circumstances seem contrary to what God has promised, continue to push, persevere, pray, and hold on to every word that God has given you. In seasons where it feels like everything is against what God said, go against the natural inclination to shut down. Instead, persevere, continue to do what God has instructed, and watch as He turns chaos into one of the greatest victories.

I encourage you not to grow weary in doing good, for in due season, you will reap a harvest if you do not give up (*Galatians 6:9*). The promise stands, but the requirement is to persist without fainting.

৵৽৵৽

Birth Out Activation Section: Appreciate Progress

As a mother progresses further in her natural pregnancy, she observes physical, emotional, and spiritual changes almost every day. Similarly, if you are attentive and sensitive to the Holy Spirit, you'll notice this is true for your spiritual journey as well. You've been recording some of these changes earlier. Take a moment to pause and reflect on how far you have come. If you haven't done so already, now is the time to acknowledge and appreciate the progress you've made on your spiritual journey. Celebrate the growth, changes, and the guidance of the Holy Spirit in shaping your path.

Have you observed anything else? In what areas do you sense the Holy Spirit guiding you?

_____

_____

_____

_____

_____

_____

_____

_____

Prayer

Dear Lord, I express my gratitude for all the changes that are unfolding within me. At times, they can be a bit intimidating, and I am thankful for the strength you provide to stay the course. I recognize it is crucial not to lose focus, and I lean on Your guidance.
In Jesus' name, I pray. Amen.
Scripture Reading: 2 Corinthians 5:17

Chapter 8

Reunited and it is ALL Good – When your Yes meets His Will!

You may think, "I didn't choose to say yes when I picked up this book and continued to read, or when I did the activities and let the Holy Spirit lead and guide me through this process." In reality, you were saying yes.

Your "yes" goes beyond a mere verbal acknowledgment. It involves your mind, will, and emotions. It involves your very soul. It goes against logic: what you see, what you experience, what you think, and what you feel. Your "yes" relies on the truth that God is the Potter, and you are the Clay. It acknowledges that God is entirely and completely in control and that we totally must surrender to Him.

Take a moment right now to examine if there are any areas in your life where you haven't fully given God your yes. Once you identify those areas, give God your answer. Not just a verbal yes, but a yes that encompasses your entire being, trusting in His plan and surrendering control.

Always remember that once you have been called, chosen, and marked by God for a purpose, your "yes" is non-negotiable. Regardless of the difficulties, agony, and lack of clarity, your affirmation of "yes" becomes a potent affirmation of your commitment to the journey and your determination to see it to the end. However, the ultimate factor that surpasses all excuses is the word of God. If He has spoken a thing, that thing is what will be.

My prayer for you is that from this day forward, you will be resolute in your commitment, casting aside every excuse that attempts to hold you back. There were moments in my personal life when it felt like nothing was going right, and I questioned if God had forsaken me. I felt far from my purpose, and the idea of redemption seemed distant. Yet, in those times of despair, distress, and discouragement, I discovered I was right in the center of God's will.

It is during moments of hardship that God reveals who or what we truly depend on, whether it be people, money, or other resources. Our allegiance must be to Him, regardless of the path He takes us through. Saying yes to God means surrendering everything into His hands, even if it involves letting go of certain people, places, or things.

Your "yes" may seem costly, and indeed, it is. It might demand everything from you. However, the most powerful aspect of this surrender is our ability to say yes, even when it feels like the cost is too high. Some might argue this cost, but I want to emphasize that this is true. It is expensive, and it will cost you everything. Nonetheless, the initial step requires self-denial and harmonizing your own will with that of God's. Just as Jesus prayed in the Garden of Gethsemane, "not my will, but yours be done."

Birth Out Activation Section: Pregnant with the Kingdom

We are all carrying something unique, designed specifically for us by the Master. Just as in a natural pregnancy, where appearance and progression can vary, our spiritual processes will also look different. The key is that we are pregnant with the Kingdom, and the focus should be on nourishing ourselves with the Word, engaging in praise and worship, and surrounding ourselves with Kingdom-minded people. Not every environment is safe for you to give birth to your ministry.

Reflecting on your journey, in what ministry areas have you sensed the Holy Spirit's guidance and prompting?

_____

_____

_____

_____

_____

_____

_____

_____

_____

Prayer

Dear Lord, help me be sensitive to people, places, and things. Please lead, guide, and direct me. I value that which You have entrusted to me and vow to protect it.

Thank you for Your wisdom.

In Jesus' Name, Amen

Scripture Reading: Luke 17:21

Chapter 9

Repositioning

The Birth Out process is all about faith. It's easy for us to say that we trust God, but when it comes down to it, do we really? I've learned that in this life, we will go through difficulties. Life will take sharp turns, and often, it's hard to figure out what God is doing. In those times when we can't see our way, we must rely on God. Personally, I'm the type of person who likes to know what's going on. I prefer having a Plan A and even a backup plan. However, this process doesn't always allow us to see what's next.

One such time for me was my family's move a few years ago to North Carolina from New York, which I mentioned earlier. Things were going smoothly for my husband and me, and our kids were about to finish high school. However, right in the middle of what was going smoothly, God interrupted our lives. This interruption was unexpected, but needed. God told us to move, and though we didn't know exactly where we were going or why, we went out of obedience. None of us had lined up a job, and the kids weren't thrilled about moving in their senior and junior years of high school. It seemed inconvenient and sort of crazy, and the things you'd want to have lined up when moving were not in place. But when God says, "Go," You Go.

This moved reminded me of Abraham when God told him to leave his father's house, his family, everything he was familiar with, and go to a place that God would show him. No wonder Abraham is the father of faith. Just imagine the level of faith it requires, abandoning everything that is familiar, comfortable, and known to venture into the unknown, solely relying on your trust in God.

So, here we were, moving to North Carolina, still uncertain about what God wanted us to do here, but knowing this is where He wanted us. Before the move, I had been teaching about the Birth Out process for several years, discussing the process of purification and the changes that take place. I thought I was an expert in that area, not realizing that God was still processing me. I now understand why my attempts to write this book earlier were unsuccessful. It was because I had to continue my Birth Out journey. I had to step into a new realm of faith and rely on it to guide me.

Although I said I trusted God, I realized during the move that I was depending on my paycheck and my husband's paycheck. I believed we could handle all the finances, but when God told us to move, I realized I didn't have the faith I thought I did. My faith was being tried. During this move, I discovered the importance of relying on God, as there was no other support available. We came to an unfamiliar state even though my parents were originally from North

Carolina, and we would visit every summer. Living here was different. In the first few months, I learned how to worship in a way I had never worshipped before, how to seek the face of God, and it was during this time that I started writing again.

The first few months, even the first year, were tough, but it was the closest I'd ever been to God. He made it clear to us He was present, had a perfect plan, and was in control of everything we were going through. The repositioning, the realignment, was all part of the process. Take a minute now to think about where you are in life and what is going on around you. Don't just focus on what's happening naturally with your job or your family; look at where you are spiritually. Before we left New York, everything secularly was great, but spiritually there was discomfort. It was like I wasn't home, even though I was in the place where I grew up. I was in the state I was familiar with, but it didn't feel like home spiritually. When we moved to North Carolina, even though everything financially was out of whack, this is where I found my spiritual home. That's what happens in this process; what may seem comfortable may really be an uncomfortable place, and what may seem uncomfortable may be the ordained place. I've learned in this process to be comfortable being uncomfortable because the moment you think things have settled is the moment that God could change, reposition, and realign you. It's okay not to know, as long as He does. One of my favorite scriptures is *Job 23:10*. During a time of uncertainty and brokenness, God gave me this scripture. He gave me his assurance that he is aware of the route I am taking and when I am tired, I will shine like pure gold. While I naturally have a personality inclined towards knowledge and planning, I am discovering that what truly matters spiritually is that God knows the path I am taking. I trust Him. My full confidence is in Him because that's the perfect position. Allow God to reposition you and watch how He blows your mind.

ಠ‍ೲಠ‍ೲ

Birth Out Activation Section:
Top of Form You're Almost There

You are on the verge of delivering the ministry (and for some ministries) that God has placed within you, but the appointed time has not yet arrived. Our character and faith still have areas that require further growth. In this spiritual pregnancy, unlike a natural one, the seed God has deposited in you (your ministry) is already developed, mature, and perfect. However, it is you who needs to undergo development and maturity to align with "Your Ministry."

This stage often becomes challenging, as impatience and weariness may set in. The desire to expedite the process becomes strong. However, it's crucial to understand that your ministry already knows the perfect time to be born. Trust in God's timing and continue your preparation. Allow Him to lead your maturation, ensuring that you fully align with the purpose He has placed within you.

Record where you are in this process. What are you feeling and thinking right now?

_____

_____

_____

_____

_____

Prayer

Father God, please help me when I get anxious and tired. I want to make sure that I am fully developed and mature so that I can be effective in ministry. I want to represent you well. Help me continue to allow You to finish the work that You have begun in me.

In Jesus' Name, Amen

Scripture Reading: Job 23:10

Chapter 10

It's All Worth It

I want to express my gratitude to you for allowing me to embark on this journey with you. Thank you for investing time in yourself and recognizing your unique, God-given purpose. Throughout this journey, I am sure that you have experienced various emotions—excitement, feeling isolated, loneliness, confusion, and even fear. It's important to acknowledge that these emotions are part of the process.

You are suited for this journey because God has chosen you specifically to carry out His plan. As we reach the end of this book, it doesn't signify the end of the process. There's always more. More training, learning, growing, maturing, and development. The focus is not on how far we have to go, but about acknowledging that God is with us on this journey.

Comparing this journey to pregnancy, it spans different durations for different individuals. The changes, contractions, and intensity may vary, but the goal is the delivery of purpose and ministry. The memory of the joy and fulfillment I experienced while holding my children after enduring labor is still vivid in my mind. It is difficult to put into words the extent of my happiness.

I could hardly contain myself. All the challenges I faced during my pregnancies and labor didn't matter anymore. It was completely worth it to spend every second with my children. Similarly, my prayer for you is that you concentrate on delivering what God has blessed you with. His anointing and purpose. It's not just for you. It's meant to bless the world. Someone is eagerly awaiting the manifestation of the purpose God has planted inside of you.

So, rather than dwelling on the pain, loss, or discomfort, concentrate on the purpose, understanding that it will all be worth it in the end.

Birth Out Activation Section: What are You Carrying?

So, what is it you are carrying, anyway? While some may already be aware, let's address any remaining questions or provide that "extra" confirmation by examining a few key points. Reflect on the areas you are passionate about. In what area(s) does God continuously use you? Disregard how comfortable you feel in these areas, as we often try to talk ourselves out of the areas God wants to use us in.

Dedicate a few moments to reflect on your life. You may be surprised to discover that you have been closer to your ministry than you think. A lot of you have probably experienced being constantly surrounded by it. I believe the Holy Spirit is revealing it to you now and will continue to do so. Don't hinder the process. Embrace your calling.

Jot down areas in ministry that you sense God has called you to.

_____

_____

_____

_____

_____

_____

Prayer

Dear Lord, thank You again for choosing me. I ask that You continue to reveal what I have been carrying. Help me embrace my call and prepare me to walk therein. I trust Your process.

In Jesus' Name, Amen

Scripture Reading: Isaiah 6:8

Chapter 11

Uniquely You

I have a message to relay to you. The Almighty God designed you in His own likeness. He was not confused when He made you, nor does He regret what He made. You matter, your journey matters, and your voice matters. You see, Birth Out is God's way of continuously giving gifts to the world. He does this through us. These gifts are valuable. Never duplicated and always relevant. Everything about who God created you to be is perfect. Let me be clear, our perfection is not about us being perfect, but it is because the perfect one lives on the inside of us.

So now, I bind the spirits of comparison, jealousy, and inadequacy that try to keep you stagnant. Some have read to this point and still feel like you are "not good enough." The truth is, you aren't, none of us are BUT God still chose us. I empathize with the challenge of resisting the urge to compare oneself to others. Most of my life, I struggled with this sometimes-crippling enemy.

In my large family, everyone has a unique characteristic that they are known as. Some examples include the funny one, the athletic one, the pretty one, the artistic one, and many more. These labels then become identities, even if it's not the one God gave you. It is easy to get wrapped up in how others perceive you. No matter how hard I tried, I just couldn't shake what I became known as. As a result, I constantly compared myself to everyone else. I used to overlook the blessings that God had given me because I constantly compared myself to others who appeared to be more talented or successful.

This brings me back to being uniquely you. No one can outdo you in being YOU. That is the one thing that only you can do. God knows us intricately and called us according to His good purpose. We don't have to compete with anyone else for our God-given purpose. It is ours and ours alone. Interestingly, just when I thought I had completed writing this book, the Holy Spirit prompted me to include an additional chapter at the very last moment. I know that there is someone reading this right now who can identify with the struggle of comparison or thinking you are not enough. Remember that God is always watching and loves you immensely, which is why I included this chapter just for you. God sees and hears you. God also wants you to know that you are called by Him. He has special plans for you and that is why you are here.

I want to offer you encouragement to keep pushing forward. Keep going. You have greatness on the inside of you that is waiting to be birthed. Can you tell me what you just felt? It's your purpose kicking, letting you know that it's there. You can and will walk in your divine purpose Through Him. You can do ALL things because He has great plans for you. You will not break; you're going to give birth.

Chapter 12

The Journey Continues

The journey is not over once you uncover your life's purpose. You are now ready to proceed to the following phase. I have added some additional activities as a bonus to taking these next steps. We've explored how to uncover our purpose.

It's intriguing how everything comes full circle. Just like how physical intimacy is significant in both the conception and birth of a baby, spiritual intimacy and worship, which we previously touched upon, are now pivotal as we approach the delivery.

Creating an atmosphere for delivery means setting the space for your spiritual seed to come forth. The process involves creating a welcoming space for God to move without hindrance, a sacred place that is spiritually pristine and uncontaminated. It is crucial to be attentive to your environment, the individuals you are in contact with, and the destinations you frequent during this period. Just as doctors advise pregnant women to limit their travel in the later stages of pregnancy, God has created a designated and sterile environment for you to give birth in. However, it is ultimately our decision to let Him be our guide to that place.

Now, let's look at what steps we should take when it's time to act on it. The following are a few bonus sections you can work through.

_____

_____

_____

_____

_____

_____

_____

_____

_____

_____

Prayer
Father God, thank you for the place that has been prepared for me to deliver. Help me stay in the mindset of worship as the delivery of my ministry is nearby. Please help me remove all hinderances and distractions so that I am ready when You say, "it is time."
In Jesus' Name, Amen
Spiritual Reading: Isaiah 43:1-2

Bonus #1

The Delivery Room

A crowded delivery room can be uncomfortable. It's essential that everyone present during the delivery serves a purpose. This isn't the time for a family reunion or social gathering. You must be willing to clear the room when the time comes for the push. Ask and write your answer to the following question. What, or who, has God been prompting you to let go of?

While having your best friend in the room might not seem like a big deal, not everyone is ready to handle the birthing process or provide you with the support. You must establish a clean and private atmosphere for the delivery. Your ministry depends on you, ready to come forth, but this can't happen just anywhere or around just anyone.

This is the moment you've been waiting for. It's time to deliver. In my opinion, this is one of the most challenging periods during pregnancy. As you eagerly await the arrival of your "baby," there are still steps to take to bring it into the world. Although this process involves discomfort, it serves a greater purpose. It's common to lose focus because of the pain and overlook the fact that it's what leads to the promise. Follow the doctor's advice and only push through the contraction. So, don't shut down now. When you feel the pressure, PUSH.

Prayer

*Father God, I
pray for discernment as I prepare to give birth. Show
me when and where you want me to give birth. I free
myself from all unnecessary attachments. Have Your
way in me. I surrender.
In Jesus' Name, Amen
Scripture Reading: Psalm 23*

Bonus #2

Walking in It

Now that it's finally here, what's the next step? It's time for you to tap into the purpose of your ministry. Begin by familiarizing yourself with it. On the lines below, ask and write.

What is it? What does it require from you? What scripture aligns with your ministry, and more importantly, what is God specifically saying to you about it? To live out your divine assignment, purpose, and calling, it is essential to seek God's will for your "baby."

Top of Form

_____

_____

_____

_____

_____

_____

_____

_____

Prayer
Father God. Help me walk boldly in that which You have called me to; show me how to use what you have given me. Always help me remember it is all for Your Glory.
In Jesus' Name, Amen
Scripture Reading: Romans 8:19

About the Author

LaTonya Parsons is a dynamic and prolific speaker with a remarkable track record of inspiring men and women to discover and pursue their God-given purpose for over two decades. Her passion lies in witnessing individuals walk boldly in their divine call, and she has dedicated her life to empowering others to embrace their unique paths.

For over twenty years, LaTonya has been at the forefront of transformational speaking, conducting workshops, seminars, and presentations that are specifically designed to propel individuals out of their comfort zones. Her approach is centered on pushing people to seek the divine will of God for their lives, encouraging them to tap into their untapped potential and purpose.

LaTonya's mission is rooted in the belief that each person has a unique purpose, and her message resonates with those seeking to discover and fulfill that purpose. With a powerful blend of passion and wisdom, she guides audiences through a journey of self-discovery, challenging them to embrace the call that God has placed on their lives.

LaTonya is a passionate advocate for individuals walking in their divine call. Her insights, gained through years of experience, provide a roadmap for those seeking spiritual fulfillment and alignment with their true purpose. Through her speaking engagements and events, she has impacted countless lives, encouraging them to step into the extraordinary and live a life that reflects their divine calling.

www.ingramcontent.com/pod-product-compliance
Lightning Source LLC
Chambersburg PA
CBHW040555010526
44110CB00054B/2708